Nigeria

Bridget Giles

Akin Oyètádé and Matthews A. Ojo, Consultants

NATIONAL GEOGRAPHIC

WASHINGTON, D.C.

Contents

Foreword

Nigeria has often been referred to as the "Giant of Africa." This stature comes from the vastness of its land, the diversity of its peoples and languages, its huge population (the largest in Africa), and the country's oil and other natural resources, which have allowed Nigeria to dominate the West African economy and its politics. Many citizens would also maintain that the continued success of its national soccer team also contributes to Nigeria's greatness!

The creation of Nigeria at the beginning of the 20th century from the merger of the colonies of Southern and Northern Nigeria can be considered a success story of British imperialism. Despite political instability and internal tensions, the country has continued to flourish.

Modern Nigeria is linked to past kingdoms and has thus become one of the centers of a new Africa linking black people in the Americas to their traditional roots. In addition, the plants, animals, and cultures are rich and diverse, and this was demonstrated when the country hosted the Second World's Festival of Black Arts and Culture in early 1977. Moreover, Nigeria's urban population has steadily modernized with a thriving entertainment industry and media.

Nevertheless, Nigeria is not a country without its problems. Its great wealth is not distributed fairly among its citizens, many of whom live under poverty. Its democratic system is still under great strain through flaws in the way elections are organized. In recent times, news reporting about Nigeria has centered on its political, ethnic, and religious crises. Deep divisions between the regions that were created long ago by religious and ethnic conflicts have recently resurfaced, often with dire con-sequences. The major problems are the sporadic clashes between

Christians and Muslims, and the violent agitation of the peoples of the Niger Delta for control of oil resources in their region.

This book, which is well researched and excellently written in a simple style, explores the richness and diversity of the history, peoples, and environment of Nigeria. It is an interesting reading for anyone eager to learn about Nigeria.

▲ Kano, Nigeria's third-largest city, is home to more than 3.5 million people. Many of its structures use traditional techniques of building with mud.

Matthews A. Ojo
Obafemi Awolowo University

Countries of the World: Nigeria

A
Land
of
Surprises

NIGERIA IS A PATCHWORK of distinctive regions, including deserts, swamps, and steamy jungles. The people of each region have traditions that link them to their lands, and one such tradition results in Nigeria's greatest spectacle. Every year the village of Argungu holds a fishing competition. Thousands of fishers from across the country line the banks of the Sokoto River. A gun is fired, and the fishers surge into the river to the sound of drums and songs. They have just one hour to catch the biggest fish. The prize is a new minibus and one million naira (about $7,900). When the competition is over, fishing is banned in that spot for the rest of the year. Fortunately the fishers have many other places to go. Nigeria has one of the largest river systems in Africa.

◀ The fishers competing in the Argungu competition work in teams of two—one carries a round gourd to help them float and the other has a hand net with hooks.

WHAT'S THE WEATHER LIKE?

The tropics are a broad band that circles the Earth at its widest point. All of Nigeria lies within the tropics. The sun shines from directly above, so the temperature is always warm. There are two seasons—the rainy season, which lasts for six to nine months, and the dry season. But the weather does vary within Nigeria. The rainy season is wettest along the coast and on the highlands. The farther north you go, the hotter it gets, the less it rains, and the longer the dry season lasts. The map opposite shows the physical features of Nigeria. Labels on this map and on similar maps throughout this book identify most of the places pictured in each chapter.

MAP KEY

Dry
☐ Semiarid

Tropical
☐ Tropical
☐ Tropical wet
☐ Tropical wet & dry

S A H E L

0   mi   200
0   km   200

Fast Facts

OFFICIAL NAME: Federal Republic of Nigeria

FORM OF GOVERNMENT: Federal Republic

CAPITAL: Abuja

POPULATION: 135,031,164

OFFICIAL LANGUAGE: English

MONETARY UNIT: Naira

AREA: 356,667 square miles (923,768 square kilometers)

BORDERING NATIONS: Benin, Cameroon, Chad, and Niger

HIGHEST POINT: Chappal Waddi 7,936 feet (2,419 meters)

LOWEST POINT: Sea level 0 feet (0 meters)

MAJOR MOUNTAIN RANGES: Cameroonian Highlands, Jos Plateau

MAJOR RIVERS: Niger and Benue

Average Temperature & Rainfall

Average High/Low Temperatures; Yearly Rainfall

Lagos (Coast):
86° F (30° C) / 75° F (24° C); 71 in (180 cm)

Jos (Central Highlands):
91° F (33° C) / 59° F (15° C); 55 in (140 cm)

Kano (Northern Plains):
91° F (33° C) / 68° F (20° C); 35 in (90 cm)

Physical Map

CHAD

Lake Chad

LAKE CHAD, page 13

Mandara Mountains

Maiduguri

NIGER

Kulmo

Shebsi Mountains

Benue

Bunga

Katsina

DESERT TRADER, page 15

Kano

BOULDERS AND HILLS, page 12

Jos

Jos Plateau

Kano

S A H E L

Sokoto

Gusau

Argungu

FISHING COMPETITION, pages 2, 6–7

Kaduna

Zaria

Kaduna

N I G E R I A

Abuja

Benue

Makurdi

Adamawa Plateau

Chappal Waddi
(Highest point in Nigeria)
7,936 ft
2,419 m

CAMEROON

Kainji Lake

Niger

WOMEN CARRYING GOURDS, page 14

Ibadan

Lokoja

Benin City

Enugu

Udi Hills

Onitsha

RIVER BOATS, page 17

Calabar

BENIN

TOGO

Lagos

CITY SCENE, page 16

RIVER BOATS, page 10

Niger Delta

Niger

Port Harcourt

Bight of Biafra

EQUATORIAL GUINEA

GHANA

Bight of Benin

Gulf of Guinea

Eurasia

Africa

NIGERIA

Atlantic Ocean

MAP KEY

⊛ National capital

● Selected city

+ Elevation

miles 0   200

km 0   200

Jungle Swamps

Nigeria has the biggest mangrove swamp in Africa and the third largest in the world. The swamp lines the sandy beaches and lagoons of the jagged Atlantic coast, stretching several miles inland. Most of it is on the gigantic Niger Delta. Mangrove trees are specially adapted to live in salty water. Their roots filter out most of the salt from the seawater. Any damaging salt that gets into the plant is washed out through holes in the leaves. The mangrove's tangled roots spread far and wide, holding the mud together and making shelters for fish. Beyond the swamps, the land is boggy but not salty. Instead, there are freshwater swamps, which provide an important habitat for birds.

BUILDING THE NIGER DELTA

You can see from this map how Nigeria's coastline bulges into the Atlantic Ocean. That bulge is the Niger Delta, the third largest delta in the world. The mighty Niger River has created this swampy river mouth over thousands of years. The river slows as it travels over the flat lowlands toward the sea, dropping the silt it has swept along from upriver. The tangled roots of mangrove trees trap the deposited dirt. This process continues to build the delta today. The river also divides into branches, so the delta is crisscrossed by hundreds of streams and creeks. As the silt continues to build up, these waterways change their routes.

In 1956 oil was discovered on the delta and now oil pipes also crisscross the land, while flames light up the night sky as oil rigs burn off unwanted natural gas. Despite this booming industry, few locals benefit, and the delta is not the easiest place to make a living.

▼ The people who live beside the Niger River rely on it for fish, shrimp, and water—for drinking and washing—but the river is becoming polluted by oil and sewage.

NIGERIA

Niger

Port Harcourt

Niger Delta

NIGER DELTA
- Beach
- Flood zones
- Mangroves
- Plains

0   mi   100

0   km   100

Thanks to cooling winds from the sea, coastal areas are not as hot as inland. But the rains fall hard, heavy, and nearly all the time from April to July. In June, the wettest month, more than 10 feet (50 cm) of rain falls. Coastal Nigerians look forward to August's "little dry" (a short dry spell). Then, there is another rainy season from September to October. Even when it is not raining, the air is humid. Even local people can find it uncomfortable, like living in a sauna.

High Plains and Hills

Traveling north from the coast, the southern lowlands merge into central hills and high plateaus. Nigeria's

JOS PLATEAU

In the middle of Nigeria is the Jos Plateau, a land of extinct volcanoes. Many rivers start their seaward journey from the plateau's flattened top and plummet down its steep southern slopes. The country's two largest rivers, the Niger and the Benue, skirt around the edge of the plateau.

The ash scattered by the volcanoes created a rich, fertile soil that is ideal for farming. The plateau also has Nigeria's most pleasant climate. It is mild and sunny. Enough rain falls from April to September to carpet the ground in short green grass, providing grazing for herds of sheep, goats, and cattle. Farmers grow yams, potatoes, millet, and sorghum in fields fenced off with cactus hedges.

For thousands of years, the Jos Plateau has been Africa's most important tin-mining region, and it is still one of the world's major suppliers of tin. Farmers find that the old mine ponds (pools used to wash the mined rocks) are useful for watering their crops.

◀ The farmland of the Jos Plateau is scattered with massive boulders and rocky outcrops.

only true mountains lie along the southern half of its eastern border with Cameroon. They are part of the Cameroonian Highlands. These highlands are some of the most beautiful and unexplored in Africa. Elsewhere, farmers have cut down most forests, but here stretches of dense forest and rich rain forest remain. The climate is hot and wet.

The remote Adamawa Plateau on the border with Cameroon is home to one of Nigeria's most important but lesser known communities, the mountain dwellers of Sukur. The Sukur people build their houses from stone and construct terraced fields on the steep slopes for planting their crops. The ancient ruins of their chief's palace look down on the village from high above. In 1999, Sukur became a United Nations

▲ Fishers paddle along a channel among the reeds of Lake Chad. The lake makes up the northeast corner of Nigeria, although in dry periods it shrinks back beyond the Nigerian border. The lake also forms parts of Niger, Chad, and Cameroon. It is mostly very shallow— no more than 23 feet (7 m) deep.

World Heritage site because of its unique culture and environment and its importance to Nigerian and African history.

Grasses Everywhere

The rest of Nigeria is mainly gently rumpled plains. Most are covered by savannas. These tropical grasslands spread out as far as the eye can see. The dry grasses are interrupted here and there by scattered trees and shrubs and patches of woodland.

The southwestern plains west of the Niger are the historic home of the Yoruba people, one of Nigeria's largest ethnic groups. The Yoruba have been farming on the plains for thousands of years. Over the last

▼ Yoruba women carry huge bundles of calabashes to market. The gourds are dried, hollowed out, and used as containers. Carrying a large or heavy load on your head is much more efficient than carrying it on your back or in your hands, because the whole body supports the weight.

several hundred years, the Yoruba have built a network of towns and villages. Before modern cities were founded in Nigeria, the country's southern plains were among the most crowded places in Africa.

The northern plains are much hotter and drier, there is little farmland, and the climate is more desert-like. There are even sand dunes in the far northwest. The Hausa and Fulani people who live there are mostly herders. They travel with herds of cattle and goats, following the rains until the start of the dry season. Each year the herders wait months for the rains to return. If the rains do not come at all, people have to sell or slaughter their animals to survive. Many herders have moved to towns such as Kano or Katsina in search of an easier life.

▲ Areas of the dry northern plains have been turned to desert by farmers growing unsuitable crops. This soil is now so dry it is used to make bricks.

▼ This trader has crossed the Sahara Desert by camel to reach the city of Katsina, in northern Nigeria.

African Metropolis

More than half of all Nigerians live in towns and cities. The best known is Lagos, which is the largest city in Africa with almost 14 million residents. This immense, fast-growing city covers several islands in a coastal lagoon, as well as parts of the mainland, all connected by bridges. Lagos Island is

the heart of the city. It was the location of the palace of the *oba* (regional ruler) for 200 years. Parts of Lagos boast high-rise buildings and comfortable homes, but much of the city is crowded—averaging six people to a room—and has poor facilities. Life is fast-paced and lively, despite high crime rates and terrible traffic jams, or "go-slows."

▼ **Lagos is a city of extremes. The downtown is filled with skyscrapers, but just a few blocks away people are living in slums.**

Like other major cities in the south, such as Port Harcourt and Calabar, Lagos is a busy trading center and a major port. Trade has always been important to Lagos. Street markets and street sellers are everywhere (especially during go-slows), and nearly anything can be bought or sold. It is not that unusual to find parts of airplanes on sale in markets!

Modern and Ancient

▲ Traditional boats
called *pinasses* carry
goods and passengers
on Nigeria's rivers.

Abuja replaced Lagos as the federal capital in 1991.
People complained that the south dominated the
government, so the capital was moved to the center of
Nigeria. Abuja was designed to function without the
chaos of Lagos. Abuja's streets
are neatly arranged and its
residents live in modern buildings.

Kano was once the center of
a city-state, a self-governing city
that rules over the surrounding
countryside. Today it is still the
main city in the north and is a
fascinating blend of old and
new. The streets of the old town
are arranged in a wheel shape,
with a market at the "hub" and
wide avenues as the "spokes."
The city wall forms the "tire."

BOAT GO-SLOWS

The country's two largest rivers, the Niger and
the Benue, have carved a giant "Y" onto the
map of Nigeria. The Niger flows around the
western edge of the Jos Plateau to meet with the
Benue, which flows around the eastern edge of the
plateau. They meet at Lokoja. There, the Niger is
nearly a mile wide. The Benue is even wider.

A lake forms where the rivers meet that is dotted
with sandbars and small islands. Lokoja is a busy port,
with boats picking up and dropping off people and
goods. The water level can sometimes be too low for
the boats to cross the sandbars. People have to either
wait for the waters to rise and float their boats, or get
out and walk!

Secrets
of the
Wild

HIGH ON NIGERIA'S SOUTHERN MOUNTAINS, the slopes are covered by thick rain forest. Clouds form a steamy haze above the treetops. The air is hot and wet. From the ground, you cannot see far since plants grow everywhere. Bushes, shrubs, and leaves cover the soil. Trees soar high above, disappearing into the mist. The greenery is broken by flashes of color—flowers, fruit, birds, and fluttering butterflies.

Suddenly, you hear a rustle. A furry black face peers out from a bush. It's a gorilla! He rests on his knuckles and chews a leaf, gazing at you with small, intelligent eyes. He is a dominant male, so his sloping back is covered by silvery fur. His troop of females and young must be nearby.

◀ Gorillas spend most of the day eating leaves, bark, herbs, and insects. In the rainy season they eat a lot of fruit.

FROM FOREST TO FARMLAND

The map opposite shows Nigeria's main vegetation zones—what grows where. Nigeria's vegetation zones roughly form broad bands that cross the country from east to west. The strip of coastal forests and swamps is replaced inland by savannas. In the past, far more forest covered Nigeria beyond the coast. In the southwest, people have cut trees down for farming or to build on the land. In the southeast, forests have been replaced by oil-palm plantations. Many trees have been cut down for lumber, too, and a great deal of that is sold abroad. Strips of forest still line rivers and streams.

Species at Risk

Nigeria is home to a broad range of plants and animals. Several, such as the Nigerian mole rat, live nowhere else on Earth. Apart from the most remote areas, people and animals are often in competition for land. People also hunt the larger animals for food. There are few national parks, but many Nigerians value nature and are campaigning for more protected areas, especially on the Niger Delta. There are nearly 400 species of animals and plants at risk in Nigeria, including lions, crocodiles, monkeys, trees, and fish.

Species at risk include:

> African lion
> African mahogany (tree)
> African sharp-nosed crocodile
> Bangwa forest warbler (bird)
> Black-crowned crane
> Black duiker (antelope)
> Cameroon greenbul (bird)
> Cheetah
> Crested genet (hunting mammal)
> Cross River gorilla
> Dama gazelle
> Ebony (tree)

> Forest elephant
> Giraffe
> Golden potto (primate)
> Goliath grouper (fish)
> Hartebeest (antelope)
> King colobus (monkey)
> Nigerian mole rat
> Small clawed otter
> Spotted eagle ray
> Spotted hyena
> West African manatee
> Western lowland gorilla
> White-throated guenon (monkey)

▼ Hartebeests are very rare African antelopes. They are unusual because their horns grow from a central bony crown on the top of their heads.

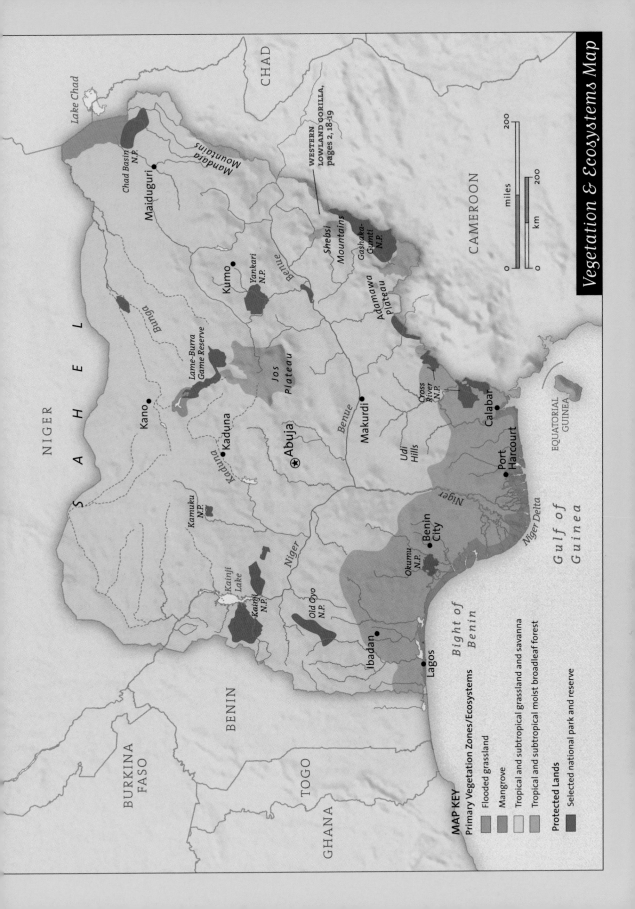

Vegetation & Ecosystems Map

CHAD

Lake Chad

NIGER

Mandara Mountains

Chad Basin N.P.

Maiduguri

WESTERN LOWLAND GORILLA, pages 2, 18-19

Shebsi Mountains

Gashaka-Gumti N.P.

Benue

Kumo

Yankari N.P.

CAMEROON

Adamawa Plateau

Bunga

Lame-Burra Game Reserve

Jos Plateau

Kano

Cross River N.P.

Kaduna

Kaduna

Abuja

Benue

Makurdi

Calabar

Udi Hills

Kamuku N.P.

Port Harcourt

EQUATORIAL GUINEA

Niger

Kainji Lake

Kainji N.P.

Niger

Benin City

Okumu N.P.

Niger Delta

BENIN

Old Oyo N.P.

Ibadan

Lagos

Bight of Benin

Gulf of Guinea

BURKINA FASO

TOGO

GHANA

scale:
0   km   200
0   miles   200

MAP KEY

Primary Vegetation Zones/Ecosystems

- Flooded grassland
- Mangrove
- Tropical and subtropical grassland and savanna
- Tropical and subtropical moist broadleaf forest

Protected Lands

- Selected national park and reserve

DISCOVERING GORILLAS

For years people thought Nigeria's gorillas had died out, but in 1987 a group of scientists were amazed to find gorillas living in the southeast. You are unlikely to see a gorilla in Nigeria, though, since scientists believe that there are fewer than 200 left, and most live in thick forests. There are two types of gorillas in Nigeria, the western lowland gorilla and the Cross River gorilla. You can tell them apart by the red patch on the lowland gorilla's forehead.

Gorillas live in small groups of five to twelve females and their young led by a male, the silverback—so called because of his silver-gray hairs. He has large canine teeth to protect his family from predators, hunters, and other males. Gorillas are peaceful animals, unless threatened. Gorillas spend a lot of time cleaning the hair of other gorillas by grooming them. The silverback is the only one that does not groom others. At night gorillas flatten plants to make soft beds. The females carry their single offspring around for months, until they can crawl. Babies also need help in finding food for several years.

▼ Duikers are small antelopes that live in African forests. They are small enough to pick their way through the thick undergrowth.

Among the Trees

Although they weigh several hundred pounds, gorillas are not the biggest forest animals. That title goes to the secretive forest elephant, which can weigh up to six tons (5.5 tonnes). That is still smaller than its cousin the savanna elephant, which now only survives in national parks. Their smaller size enables forest elephants to live in the dense rain forest. They are also a little darker, so they are better hidden among the trees. Forest elephants have straighter tusks since curved ones might get caught on vegetation. Little is known about their habits.

Forest elephants clear paths that many other forest dwellers use. Cross River National Park alone is home to at least 1,500 forest species. Monkeys and squirrels climb the trees in search of fruit and seeds. On the ground, bush pigs snuffle for juicy shoots. Small, shy antelope called duikers browse leaves, shoots, and fruits. Duikers live alone or pair up for life, but there are larger antelope such as bongos and bushbucks that live in small herds of ten or fewer. At night catlike civets and genets hunt for smaller animals, while bush babies such as the golden potto snack on insects and fruits.

▲ A family of forest elephants drink from a waterhole. The red color of their skin comes from rolling in mud.

▼ Pottos are skilled climbers with strong hands and a firm grip.

Life on the Savanna

Many years ago Nigeria's savannas teemed with giraffes, elephants, lions, cheetahs, and large herds of antelope. Today, most of these animals have

SWAMP NURSERIES AND MERMAIDS

The muddy waters of a mangrove swamp do not look welcoming to wildlife. The mangrove trees form tightly packed thickets, and no other plants can grow in the salty water. Yet mangroves are a haven for marine animals and nesting birds. Underwater the branching roots protect young fish, sea turtles, reptiles, shrimp, and lobsters from oceangoing predators such as tuna and dolphins. Crocodiles wait patiently for animals to emerge from the tangled roots. The rare West African manatee gracefully raises its head to graze on overhanging mangroves or get a breath of fresh air. Some people think that the manatee gave rise to stories about mermaids. Fishers on the Niger Delta tell tales of a sea goddess or mermaid called Mami Water. She is beautiful and generous but jealous and dangerous if crossed. Manatees were hunted for their meat and for use in traditional medicines, so they are now protected by law.

been killed by hunters or their habitats have been destroyed. So Nigerians and tourists from abroad travel to remote Yankari National Park to see the few remaining animals. Visitors to the park can also enjoy swimming in Wikki Warm Springs, where warm water bubbles up from a hole in the ground.

▼ A pangolin laps up some river water. The tongue is almost as long as its body.

Outside national parks, baboons still live in large troops of ten or more animals. These big monkeys can find plants to eat nearly anywhere—in trees, on the ground, and underground. They also raid people's trash and crops and hunt small antelope, mammals, and birds.

Armored Attacker

The oddest savanna dweller is the pangolin. Instead of being covered in fur like other mammals, the pangolin has scales. When alarmed, it rolls into an armor-plated ball. The pangolin uses its long, sticky tongue to lick up ants and termites, which are abundant on the plains.

Some savannas are like termite cities, covered by mounds of soil built by the insects. Some mounds are taller than a person. Inside the mounds termites live in complex societies that look after a gigantic queen while she lays thousands of eggs each day. The pangolin can break open a termite mound by leaning on it, resting its weight on its tail, and then ripping into the mound with its front claws.

A HOUSE OF THORNS

Thorny acacias are common savanna trees. Giraffes browse on them from below, trimming the trees into distinctive umbrella shapes. Some acacias have tiny defenders who help scare off plant munchers. Communities of ants live inside the trees' thorns, which they hollow out when the thorns are green and soft. In addition to homes, the acacia provides its guests with food. In return, the ants will march together on browsers and grazers, biting them into retreat.

▲ An ant carries a bud-like leaf back into its nest to feed the larvae.

Unearthing *the* Past

I N 1954 A NIGERIAN WAS MINING TIN on the Jos Plateau, near the village of Nok, when he found something completely unexpected. He unearthed a life-size head. The head was made from baked clay, or terra-cotta. Its sculptor had not shaped a realistic head but had molded the clay into an artistic representation of a man. The miner knew he had found something important as well as beautiful, but he had no idea how important until the head was studied by archaeologists. Scientists figured out that it was about 2,000 years old. Since then, people have searched the area around Nok carefully. Many terra-cotta sculptures have been found—heads, whole figures, and sculpted animals, too. The sculptures of the Nok culture are the oldest ever found south of the Sahara Desert.

◄ Every terra-cotta head made by the Nok people is different. Archaeologists believe that each was sculpted individually rather than cast in a mold.

ONE NATION, MANY STATES

▲ Nigerian chiefs dressed in traditional clothing that shows their high rank gather at a political rally in southern Nigeria.

The nation of Nigeria has existed for nearly 100 years. Toward the end of the 1800s and the early 1900s, the British took control of several West African kingdoms and empires. They divided some up and joined others to create the British-ruled colony of Nigeria. Yet Africans had been founding kingdoms and city-states and forging empires in what is now Nigeria for hundreds of years. So although the state of Nigeria is fairly new, the country's history stretches back for thousands of years. Nigeria's ancient kingdoms no longer exist, but there are still many Nigerian kings and emirs (Muslim commanders or princes). They have little formal political power, and their roles are largely ceremonial, but they still have influence among their people.

Time line

This chart shows the significant dates of developments in the area which later became the independent nation of Nigeria.

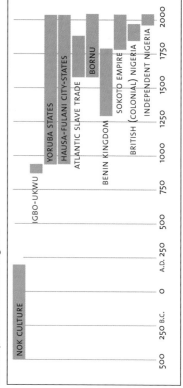

NOK CULTURE

IGBO-UKWU

YORUBA STATES

HAUSA-FULANI CITY-STATES

ATLANTIC SLAVE TRADE

BENIN KINGDOM

BORNU

SOKOTO EMPIRE

BRITISH (COLONIAL) NIGERIA

INDEPENDENT NIGERIA

500 B.C.   250 B.C.   0   A.D. 250   500   750   1000   1250   1500   1750   2000

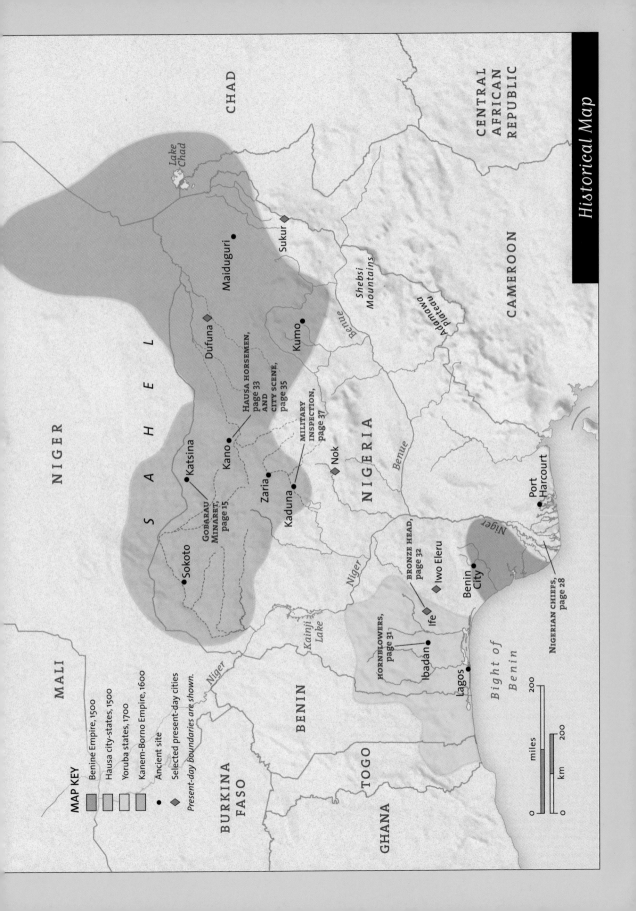

MAP KEY

Benine Empire, 1500
Hausa city-states, 1500
Yoruba states, 1700
Kanem–Borno Empire, 1600

• Ancient site
◆ Selected present-day cities

Present-day boundaries are shown.

MALI

NIGER

BURKINA
FASO

GHANA

TOGO

BENIN

S A H E L

Niger

• Sokoto

GOBARAU
MINARET,
page 15

• Katsina

• Kano

HAUSA HORSEMEN,
page 33
AND
CITY SCENE,
page 35

◆ Dufuna

Maiduguri •

Lake
Chad

CHAD

◆ Sukur

Shebsi
Mountains

Benue

Kumo •

Zaria •

Kaduna •

MILITARY
INSPECTION,
page 37

◆ Nok

NIGERIA

Benue

Adamawa
Plateau

CAMEROON

CENTRAL
AFRICAN
REPUBLIC

Niger

Kainji
Lake

HORNBLOWERS,
page 31

Ibadan •

Lagos •

BRONZE HEAD,
page 32

◆ Ife

◆ Iwo Eleru

Benin
City

NIGERIAN CHIEFS,
page 28

Port
Harcourt •

Niger

*Bight of
Benin*

0   200
miles

0   200
km

Stone Age to Iron Age

Hundreds of thousands of years ago ancient Nigerian people learned to make tools from sharp pieces of hard rock. They ate the plants and animals they found or caught in the wild. Gradually, they learned how to farm and keep animals. Oil palms and yams were likely the first crops they grew.

Nigerians still use the wood and leaves of oil palms to build houses and fires. The leaves are also used to make ropes and clothing. The oil is great for cooking, and the sap can be turned into wine.

▲ Yams have been farmed in Nigeria for at least 3,000 years.

BOATS AND BONES

In 1987 an ancient boat was dug up in the northeast, near Dufuna village. The accidental discoverer was a Fulani herder digging a well. The boat was an elegantly shaped wooden dugout with pointed ends. The Dufuna Canoe is around 8,000 years old, making it the oldest in Africa and the third oldest in the world. It dates back to the Stone Age, when people used stone tools.

But why was a boat found in such a dry part of Nigeria? The north was much wetter thousands of years ago. Lake Chad was so much bigger that archaeologists have named it Megachad. They have found the remains of ancient villages near the shores of Megachad, including a 4,000-year-old house.

The Dufuna Canoe is not the earliest evidence of people living in Nigeria. In 1965 a 10,000-year-old human skeleton was found in a rain forest rock shelter near Iwo Eleru, in Ondo State. Stone tools 12,000 years old have also been found at Iwo Eleru and elsewhere.

Yams are hardy root crops that grow nearly anywhere. People probably searched for wild yams before discovering how to grow their own in large numbers. Perhaps early farmers noticed how yams sprouted from the remains of meals.

Near Kano, rock paintings of cattle prove that people

were keeping animals there 2,500 years ago.

The people who founded the Nok culture were skilled sculptors and knew how to purify iron and work it into complicated shapes, such as tools and jewelry. The furnaces of Nok ironworkers date back 2,500 years.

The First Towns

Yoruba farmers were the first to live in towns. The city of Ife (or Ile-Ife) was founded around A.D. 900. Each city was shaped like a wheel, surrounded by a wall. People lived within the walls but traveled outside to tend their land. Over time several towns became powerful kingdoms. The Yoruba kings ruled with the help of palace officials, town chiefs, and state councils. Court artists created beautiful artwork, including brass and terra-cotta masks and blue glass beads. The king of Oyo had a 1,000-strong cavalry, using horses from north of the Sahara Desert. The cavalry helped make Oyo a powerful empire in the 1600s and 1700s.

▲ This Yoruba bronze armlet—worn above the elbow—has a human face cast on the side.

◀ Hornblowers, along with drummers and men shaking rattles, announce the presence of the alafin— the ruler of the empire of Oyo.

City of the Gods

Ife is a sacred city according to the Yoruba religion. Yoruba legend says that Ife was not only the first Yoruba city, but also the place of Earth's creation. The great god Olodumare threw an iron chain down from the heavens, and his son Oduduwa climbed down the chain to the water below. He took with him a calabash full of sand, which became the Earth, the nut of an oil palm, and a chicken. The leaves of the palm tree that grew from the nut represent the many other Yoruba cities that grew out of the traditions of Ife. Each Yoruba city has its own legends, often involving a prince from Ife founding the city.

▲ Ife is renowned for its bronze sculptures. This head is probably of a ruler, or *oni*. Hair may have been attached to the holes around the mouth to form a beard.

A People Without Leaders

In the southeast, between the Niger Delta and the eastern highlands live the Igbo people. They have a saying that the "Igbo have no kings." Yet at Igbo-Ukwu a man digging to build a house discovered 1,200-year-old graves. They were filled with a wealth of goods, and the bones of what may be a long-buried king. The treasures included glass and stone beads, decorated armor, jewelry, a crown, and weapons. Some of these treasures had come from as far away as Europe.

Even if they were the graves of kings, it is true that many Igbo societies had no single ruler. Instead, elected councils of both men and women led the community. Only the most respected members of a community made it onto a council: People who had been successful in life or business, or

were considered wise. Igbo people are still known for rewarding and encouraging individual achievements.

▲ A Fulani boy watches over a herd of cows. The Fulani once traveled with their herds but most of them now live in towns.

City-State to Empire

In the north, Hausa and Fulani people had organized several towns by A.D. 1000. The Hausa were traders. Some owned herds of cattle, too. Their cattle were looked after by Fulani herders, along with their own

▼ Hausa horsemen ride out of Kano following a Muslim festival.

animals. People grew rich buying goods brought across the Sahara Desert, selling them to each other, and to traders traveling south. Weapons, horses, and salt were imported. Cloth, leather, slaves, and gold were exported. By 1350 several towns were so wealthy and powerful that they were independent city-states ruled by emirs. They included Kano, Katsina, and Zaria.

BENIN BRONZES

▲ The oba's mother was called the queen mother. Sculptures of her were placed on palace altars.

Legend says that the city and kingdom of Benin were founded by a Yoruba prince, although the citizens of Benin were Edo people. Benin's golden era lasted from the 1400s to the 1700s. Its court artists produced thousands of stunning brass sculptures (often called bronzes). The artists sculpted heads from the soft metal. They were usually heads of enemy kings or other rulers who had been defeated in battle. On hundreds of brass wall plaques, court artists etched and molded scenes celebrating the success and wealth of Benin, its soldiers, and its obas (kings) in battle and at court.

Trade also brought the Islamic religion from North Africa, around 1,000 years ago. The Hausa city-states became important Islamic states as well as centers of learning and culture. In the 1800s a Muslim cleric named Usman dan Fodio united the city-states into the Sokoto empire. He wanted to improve life for all Muslims, both rich and poor. His revolutionary empire became the biggest in West Africa and spread Islam far and wide.

A Cruel Trade

Trade was important to all these states and people. In the 1400s the Portuguese became the first Europeans to join in when they began trading along the coast. They were followed by Dutch, French, and British traders. By the 1600s Europeans were buying slaves to work the land in their new American colonies. American merchants joined the trade in the 1800s.

Slavery was not new to Africa. However, in Africa, slaves or their descendants were generally absorbed into their masters' community and eventually became free members of society. The Europeans expanded the slave trade to a scale never seen before.

While some Africans made a profit, many more suffered greatly. At least 3.5 million people were enslaved and shipped across the Atlantic from what

▼ **People leave the central mosque in Kano after Friday prayers. The mosque has room for 10,000 worshippers.**

is now Nigeria. Many died on the crossing. If they lived, they faced a life of hardship and suffering as slaves. The cruel trade continued until slavery was abolished, or made illegal, in Britain (1834) and the United States (1865).

▲ A Calabar chief with his sons in the early 1900s. The chief ruled a region of southeastern Nigeria in name only. The British governors held the power.

Foreign Rule

By the late 1800s Europeans no longer used slaves. Instead they wanted places to sell the goods being made by their new factories at home. And they wanted cheap raw materials—such as palm oil for lubricating machinery and making soap. To control this new trade, Britain waged war on the Yoruba and Benin kingdoms, the Sokoto empire, the Igbo people, and all their neighbors. Despite great resistance, some rulers were defeated in battle; others were tricked with treaties, not realizing they had signed away control of their empires. The war lasted from 1885 to 1906. In 1914, the Colony and Protectorate of Nigeria was formed under the control of a British governor general.

SLAVERY BESTSELLER

In 1756 a young Igbo boy was captured by slave raiders and shipped across the Atlantic. Olaudah Equiano saw many horrors on the journey across the Atlantic, and faced more on arrival in the Americas. He remained a slave until he managed, through careful saving and trading, to buy his way to freedom. In 1789 he published a book about his life, *The Interesting Narrative of the Life of O. Equiano*, which became a bestseller and made Equiano wealthy. It is one of the earliest books published by a black African writer. Equiano became an important figure in the abolitionist, or antislavery, movement.

Freedom Fighters

Nigerians did not like British rule. They were given the worst jobs, working for little money. Everyone had to pay taxes to their foreign rulers. If they could not find work, they had to grow cash crops (such as groundnuts) to earn money. Yet they were not allowed to vote or have a say in how their country was ruled. People started to complain, campaign, and fight. During the 1928–29 Women's War, women staged protests

▼ Nigerian troops are inspected by the British lieutenant governor, a senior administrative official during colonial times.

against British rule, often singing and dancing all night to poke fun at the British. When the women burned down factories, hundreds were shot dead.

Later, many nationalist leaders emerged across the country, representing different groups of people. When Nigeria finally gained independence in 1960, Tafawa Balewa, a Muslim from the north of the country, became prime minister.

Celebrating Life

IT'S AN IMPORTANT DAY IN Kano—a big Muslim festival is being celebrated. The streets of this 1,000-year-old city are lined with spectators. People have already attended public prayers outside the city. Now they fill the streets to see the emir, with his scores of horsemen, wrestlers, and lute players, parade through Old Town to the public square. The horsemen and their horses wear ornately patterned costumes. The emir receives the salutes of his cavalry, who gallop across the square at top speed, halting steps away to salute him with their drawn swords. Music, dancing, and singing follow through the night. This is Kano's yearly Sallah Durbar, or military parade. Other northern cities, such as Katsina, also hold *durbars*.

◀ **Spectators gather as young Hausa men engage in a mock fight during the Sallah Durbar in Kano.**

GROWING URBAN POPULATION

The population of Nigeria has grown rapidly in the last 15 years. In 1991 the country had about 90 million people, in 2006 there were more than 130 million. Almost half the population is under 15 years of age. This is one of the fastest rates of growth in the world, making it hard for the government to provide enough education and employment. In 1970, 20 percent of the population lived in cities. As the map opposite shows, almost half of Nigerians now live in urban areas.

Forecasters expect this figure to rise to 65 percent by 2025. Although there have been towns and cities in Nigeria for hundreds of years, in the last century the number of urban Nigerians has increased dramatically. This is partly due to job opportunities created when the oil industry expanded.

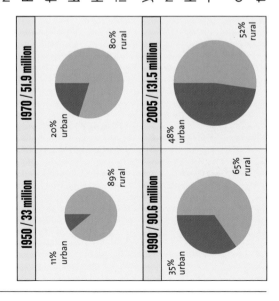

1950 / 33 million
11% urban
89% rural

1970 / 51.9 million
20% urban
80% rural

1990 / 90.6 million
35% urban
65% rural

2005 / 131.5 million
48% urban
52% rural

Common Phrases

There are hundreds of languages spoken in Nigeria—at least 250, and perhaps more than 400. Most Nigerians learn to speak more than one language. In the southwest many people speak Yoruba. In the north many people speak Hausa, which has been widely used by traders across West Africa for centuries. In the southeast, the Igbo form another large language group. Here are some words and phrases you might hear in Nigeria:

Yoruba phrases

Good morning	E kaaaro
Thank you	E shee
Yes	Beni
No	Oti

Hausa phrases

Hello	Sannu
Thank you	Na gode
Yes	I (ee)
No	A'a (ah uh)

Igbo phrases

Good day	Ezigbo ubosi
Thank you	Dalu
Yes	Ehe
No	Mba

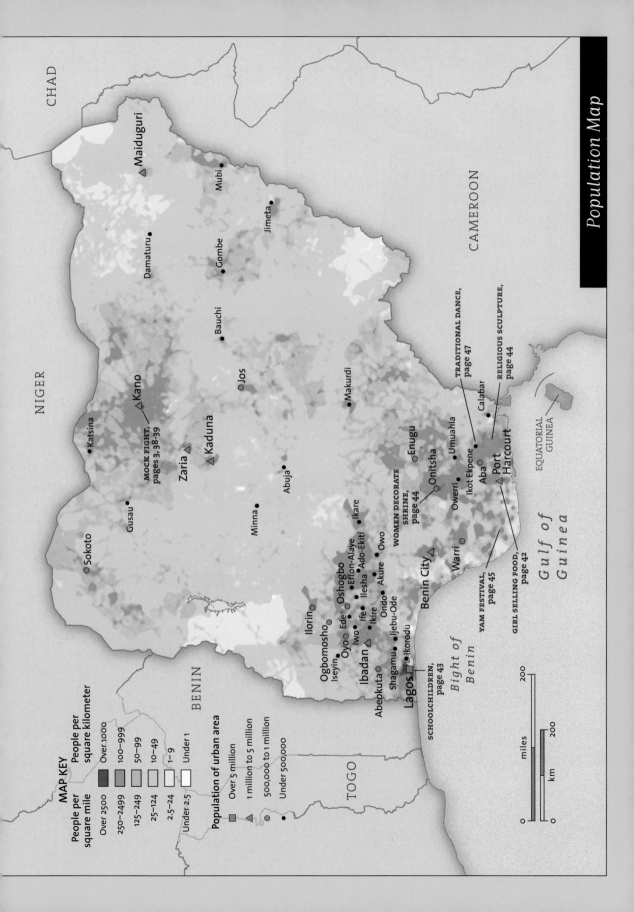

Population Map

MAP KEY

People per square mile	People per square kilometer
Over 2500	Over 1000
250–2499	100–999
125–249	50–99
25–124	10–49
2.5–24	1–9
Under 2.5	Under 1

Population of urban area

Over 5 million
1 million to 5 million
500,000 to 1 million
Under 500,000

CHAD

NIGER

CAMEROON

BENIN

TOGO

EQUATORIAL GUINEA

Gulf of Guinea

Bight of Benin

△ Maiduguri
• Mubi
• Damaturu
Jimeta •
• Gombe
• Bauchi
• Katsina
• Sokoto
• Gusau
△ Kano
○ Jos
• Minna
△ Zaria
△ Kaduna
• Abuja
• Makurdi
• Ilorin
Ogbomosho ○
Iseyin •
Oyo ○
Iwo •
Ede •
Oshogbo
Effon-Alaye
Ilesha •
Ife •
Ado-Ekiti
Ikare •
Ikire •
Owo •
Ondo •
Akure •
Ijebu-Ode •
Shagamu •
Abeokuta ○
△ Ibadan
Ikoredu •
Lagos
○ Enugu
○ Onitsha
• Owerri
Umuahia •
Ikot Ekpene •
Aba ○
△ Port Harcourt
Calabar •
Warri ○
Benin City △

SCHOOLCHILDREN, page 43

GIRL SELLING FOOD, page 42

YAM FESTIVAL, page 45

WOMEN DECORATE SHRINE, page 44

RELIGIOUS SCULPTURE, page 44

TRADITIONAL DANCE, page 47

MOCK FIGHT, pages 3, 38–39

miles
0   200

km
0   200

Many children work to help their families, like this potato-seller.

Life Is Hard

For many Nigerians, life is a daily struggle. At least 60 percent are below the poverty line (living on less than a dollar a day).

Each year in the countryside, farmers and herders worry that it will not rain enough. To make life easier, rural people often pull together through tough times. They help each other when it is harvest time, knowing that the favor will be returned. Children have many chores. Girls help with cooking, washing, and fetching water, as well as working in the fields cultivating crops such as rice or yams. Boys help with farming, herding, and building. Because they are so busy, and because education is not always free, it is difficult for some children to go to school regularly.

Since there are not enough jobs to go around and housing is limited, life can also be difficult in cities. As in the countryside, people do their best to help themselves. Many city dwellers create their own

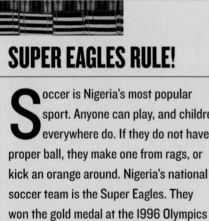

SUPER EAGLES RULE!

Soccer is Nigeria's most popular sport. Anyone can play, and children everywhere do. If they do not have a proper ball, they make one from rags, or kick an orange around. Nigeria's national soccer team is the Super Eagles. They won the gold medal at the 1996 Olympics in Atlanta. The women's national team, the Super Falcons, won the African Championships for the fifth time in 2006.

opportunities. They might start a small business selling homemade sweets or soap, for example.

Large Families

Family is very important to Nigerians. Children are taught to respect their beginning at an early age. Families tend to be large, with many brothers, sisters, and cousins. Everyone in the family, and the wider community, helps look after the children.

Men can marry more than one wife. A man, his wives, and their children, as well as some elderly relatives, live together in a compound (a group of buildings around a central courtyard). Each wife or elder has his or her own house within the compound.

The children live with their mother. The wives take turns cooking for their husband. The husband gives his wives money for food, but they also earn money for themselves and their children so that they do not rely solely on their

NATIONAL HOLIDAYS

Nigeria's national holidays include the major Christian and Muslim festivals. The dates of Eid el-Kabir (the end of the Hajj season of pilgrimage), Eid al-Fitr (the end of Ramadan, a month of daylight fasting), and the Prophet's Birthday (celebrating the birth of Muhammad) change every year because Muslim festivals follow the phases of the moon. There are also numerous local festivals.

JANUARY	New Year's Day
MARCH-APRIL	Good Friday, Easter Sunday, and Easter Monday
MAY 1	Worker's Day
MAY 29	Democracy Day
OCTOBER 1	Independence Day
DECEMBER 25	Christmas Day
DECEMBER 26	Boxing Day

▼ Students crowd into a Lagos classroom. Nigerian girls tend to stay in school for fewer years than boys.

husband. They might have some land that they farm, or run a small business.

In northern towns and cities, Muslim women lead more sheltered lives. They might need to make some extra money but can rarely leave the home without a male relative. So their children help with chores outside the home, like shopping. Or, they might sell their mother's homemade foods at the market.

▲ The Ibibio people from southern Nigeria make sculptures to represent the spirits of their ancestors.

▼ Igbo women come together to decorate the village shrine.

Many Beliefs

Spiritual and family life overlap in Nigeria. The honor and respect people have toward their ancestors is as much a part of their religion as the god or gods they worship. Most Nigerians are either Christian or Muslim, but African religions are still practiced at the same time. Many Yoruba and Igbo people are Christian, but they likely keep a small shrine at home to honor their personal god, or *chi*. There are many Yoruba *orisha* (gods and goddesses), each associated with particular things. Ogun, the orisha of war and iron, is now also the god of people who use iron or steel to make a living, including taxi and truck drivers. A Christian Yoruba might still honor or pray to the orisha, as a Roman Catholic does the saints.

Art Everywhere

In Nigeria art is not something that people only see at a museum or gallery. Instead, artwork is put to use in all areas of life: as furniture, parts of houses, decoration, tools, weapons, symbols of power or religion, clothing, and masks and costumes for dancers in parades. Alongside roads and highways are shrines containing carved figures of ancestors, gods, or spirits.

Artists work with metal, wood, clay, or whatever materials they can find, even cement. In the past,

YUMMY YAMS

In the southern half of Nigeria, where people farm the land, yams are a staple food, along with cassava and rice. Like potatoes, yams are root crops. But they are much bigger than potatoes, more tubular, and have a thick barklike skin. People cook them in many ways, including grinding or pounding and boiling or frying. Yams are great for eating with other foods, such as sauces and stews containing spices, onions, vegetables, peanuts, and meat. Nigerians, especially in the south, like spicy food.

▲ In August, villagers celebrate the New Yam festival to mark the start of a new work year.

OSHUN'S SACRED FOREST

On the outskirts of the city of Oshogbo is a forest that is home to Oshun, the Yoruba goddess of love and fertility. People have built shrines and temples for Oshun in the forest. The fairytale buildings are sculpted from cement in a style that is both ancient and modern. Every year people gather for a festival held in Oshun's honor. Every Yoruba settlement used to have a nearby sacred grove, but few of them remain.

▼ Worshipers gather in the Oshogbo forest during the Oshun festival. They make offerings to the goddess by dropping pigeons, snails, and other objects into the river that flows through the forest.

Yoruba woodcarvers made elaborate posts for the houses of chiefs and kings. Today artists carve doors for offices or hospitals, with scenes from modern life.

Great Writers

Olaudah Equiano was the first of many world-famous Nigerian authors. In 1958 Chinua Achebe's first novel *Things Fall Apart* was published. It explores the arrival of white missionaries in an Igbo village and their impact on village society and culture. His book has had a major influence on other African writers and it is studied in schools across the continent and around the world.

In 1986 Nigerian writer Wole Soyinka became the first black African to win the Nobel Prize for literature. He has written many plays, novels, and books about what it means to be African today. He has also been an outspoken critic of the rulers of Nigeria. As a result,

he has spent time both in prison and in exile, banned from his own country.

Making Music

Lagos has one of Africa's largest music scenes. One of Nigeria's most famous modern-day musicians was Fela Ransome Kuti. He was the creator of Afrobeat, which combines African music and jazz, using both traditional and modern instruments. Kuti's music was often fast and furious. He raged against injustice in his songs and became very popular. He was imprisoned by the government for a short while. When he died in 1997, a million people filled the streets of Lagos for his funeral procession, which took seven hours to travel the 20 miles (32 km) to his burial place.

▲ Annang boys perform a traditional dance in masks and headresses. They remain silent to conceal their identities.

▼ Fela Kuti performs at a charity concert in 1986.

Giant
of
West
Africa

PEOPLE CALL NIGERIA THE GIANT of West Africa. That is not just because it is the biggest country with the largest population in the region, but because it is also the most important politically and economically. Nigeria is richer than all the other West African nations, and it holds considerable power. It is a key player in the Economic Community of West African States (ECOWAS). Nigeria provides most of the money and soldiers for the organization's armed peacekeeping force, which helped bring peace to Liberia and Sierra Leone when the rest of the world did not want to get involved. Yet the path to prosperity has not been easy, and many Nigerians still live in poverty despite all the money Nigeria has made from oil.

◀ **A workman makes repairs to equipment on an oil drilling platform off the coast of Nigeria. To many Nigerians, oil has proven to be a curse instead of a blessing.**

STATE POLITICS

Nigeria is a federal republic. The country is divided into 36 states and the federal capital territory of Abuja. Every state has a capital and its own government headed by a state governor. Sometimes state governors disagree with the federal government. In 2006 Ekiti state was placed under military rule when the governor was removed from office for corruption, or using his position for personal financial gain. Most states have their own radio and television stations. Politicians have used advertising jingles and specially written dramas to encourage people to vote.

▼ Nigeria's press is thriving, with more than 100 national and local newspapers on sale in addition to international papers and magazines.

Trading Partners

Nigeria's most important export is oil, more than half of which is shipped to the United States. Rubber and cacao (for chocolate and cocoa) are the next most important exports. But the quantities of cocoa and rubber exported are tiny compared to the shipments of oil, which account for 95 percent of all exports. Nigeria imports machinery, chemicals, transportation equipment, manufactured goods, food, and live animals.

Country	Percentage Nigeria exports
United States	52.5%
Spain	8.2%
Brazil	6.1%
All others combined	33.2%

Country	Percentage Nigeria imports
China	10.4%
United States	7.3%
United Kingdom	6.7%
Netherlands	6.0%
France	5.9%
All others combined	63.7%

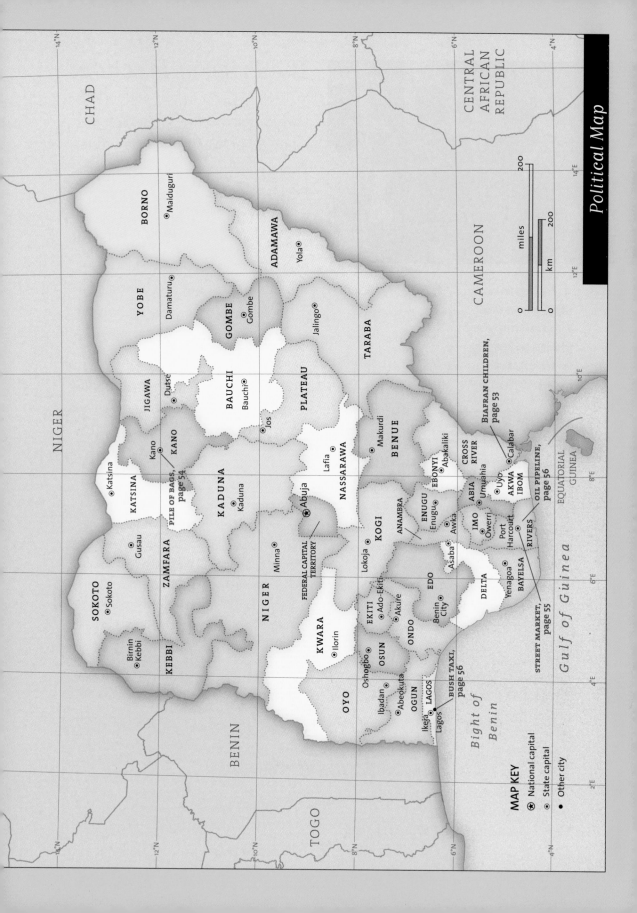

CHAD

NIGER

BENIN

TOGO

BORNO
●Maiduguri

ADAMAWA
Yola●

YOBE
Damaturu●

GOMBE
Gombe●

BAUCHI
Bauchi●

JIGAWA
Dutse●

Jalingo●

TARABA

KANO
Kano●

PLATEAU

Jos●

KATSINA
Katsina●

KADUNA
Kaduna●

Makurdi●

BENUE

Lafia●

NASSARAWA

CROSS
RIVER
Calabar●

ZAMFARA

Gusau●

Abuja⊛

FEDERAL CAPITAL
TERRITORY

KOGI

ANAMBRA

ENUGU
Enugu●

EBONYI
Abakaliki●

ABIA
Umuahia●

AKWA
IBOM
Uyo●

SOKOTO
Sokoto●

KEBBI

Birnin
Kebbi●

NIGER

Minna●

Lokoja●

Awka●

IMO
Owerri●

Port
Harcourt●

RIVERS

OIL PIPELINE,
page 56

EQUATORIAL
GUINEA

Asaba●

KWARA
Ilorin●

EKITI
Ado-Ekiti●

Akure●

ONDO

EDO
Benin
City●

DELTA

Yenagoa●

BAYELSA

OYO

OSUN
Oshogbo●

Ibadan●

OGUN
Abeokuta●

LAGOS
Ikeja●
Lagos●

BUSH TAXI,
page 56

STREET MARKET,
page 55

BIAFRAN CHILDREN,
page 53

PILE OF BAGS,
page 54

CAMEROON

CENTRAL
AFRICAN
REPUBLIC

Gulf of Guinea

Bight of
Benin

MAP KEY
⊛ National capital
● State capital
● Other city

miles
0   200

km
0   200

▲ President Obasanjo (right) with the singer Bono and several other international figures at the World Economic Forum in 2005.

The Price of Freedom

In 1960 Nigeria won independence from Britain, at the same time as many other West African countries. There were huge celebrations. People looked forward to life without foreign rulers telling them what to do and denying them the right to vote. However, since independence Nigeria has suffered at the hands of several native rulers. There have been years when the army ran the country, taking and keeping power by force. At other times, politicians seemed to run the country for personal profit. The term "squandermania"

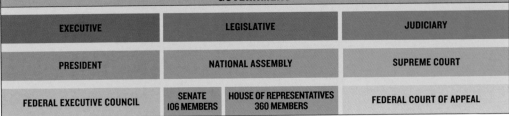

HOW THE GOVERNMENT WORKS

After years of military rule, Nigeria adopted a new constitution in 1999. Everyone above the age of 18 is allowed to vote. Voters elect the president and members of the National Assembly. The National Assembly is made up of two houses: the Senate and the House of Representatives. The president has a lot of power, being both the head of the government and the leader of the National Assembly, and also the person who chooses Supreme Court judges. The president and the Federal Executive Council run the country. In 2006 the National Assembly threw out a bill that would have allowed President Obasanjo to stay in office for a third four-year term.

GOVERNMENT			
EXECUTIVE	LEGISLATIVE		JUDICIARY
PRESIDENT	NATIONAL ASSEMBLY		SUPREME COURT
FEDERAL EXECUTIVE COUNCIL	SENATE 106 MEMBERS	HOUSE OF REPRESENTATIVES 360 MEMBERS	FEDERAL COURT OF APPEAL

BLOODY CIVIL WAR

Nigeria's first military coup, or takeover, came just six years after independence. There had been riots about how many government seats each part of the country could hold. The army overthrew the government, promising to keep the peace. But Colonel Ojukwu, the military ruler of the Igbo lands in the east, refused to accept the new leaders. In 1967 he declared the independent republic of Biafra. The military government tried to stamp out the rebellion. The Igbo resisted for three long years before they were defeated. Three million Biafrans died—in battle, from starvation, or from disease.

▲ Starving Biafran children wait patiently for relief workers to bathe and feed them. The military government cut off all supplies to the region during the war.

was coined in Nigeria to describe how politicians grew rich while the poor got poorer.

Yet ordinary Nigerians continued to fight to improve their country, speaking out and demonstrating against corruption and unfair rulers. Many have spent time in prison or in exile, for standing up for civil rights. Others have died. In 1999 the first democratic elections in 20 years were held. The winner was Olusegun Obasanjo. In 2003 and 2007 more elections were held. In 2007, a democratically elected civilian president (Obasanjo) handed over power to another, Alhaji Umaru Musa Yar, for the first time since independence. Each time reforms have been made to make the process more fair.

INDUSTRY MAP

This map shows Nigeria's main centers of industry and mining. Most of the country's natural resources are in the south, which has led to conflicts over the distribution of profits.

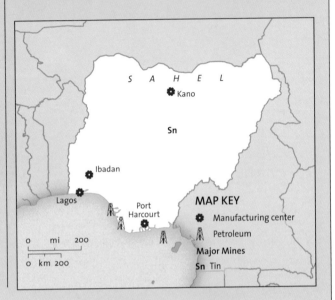

S A H E L

❀ Kano

Sn

❀ Ibadan

❀ Lagos

Port
Harcourt

o   mi   200

o km 200

MAP KEY

❀ Manufacturing center

⛏ Petroleum

Major Mines

Sn Tin

▼ A pyramid rises above Kano. It is not made from stones, but from sacks of groundnuts, an important Nigerian crop.

Making a Living

Over two-thirds of Nigerians make their living from the land, either by farming, herding, or fishing. However, most farms are small and scattered and do not produce enough food to feed the growing population. For now, Nigeria has to import food, but the government is encouraging farmers to form cooperative societies to help them grow and sell more produce.

Many people cannot find paid employment, especially in the cities, so they create their own opportunities, setting up market stalls or walking the streets selling a vast array of goods—from clothespins and dishcloths to medicine and electronic gadgets—to residents and

motorists alike. Many women, particularly in the south, run market stalls. Trading is a good way for women to earn money because they can combine their business with looking after the children and preparing the evening meal.

Bike and Bush Taxis

Many men buy cheap automobiles, motorcycles, or minibuses and set up unofficial taxi businesses—known as bush taxis. Outside of towns the taxi might be a truck with rows of benches for seats. Passengers are picked up on the side of the street and all contribute toward the fare. People say that bush taxis

▲ Shoppers crowd the stalls of Port Harcourt's Flyover Market. Economic experts believe that about 40 percent of the country's economy is unregulated and untaxed because people create their own jobs.

are crowded, too fast, and dangerous, but they are vital to urban life. In Abuja *okadas* (motorcycle taxis) have been banned because the governor claimed they were involved in too many accidents. Bush taxis have also been used as getaway cars by armed robbers. Yet without bush taxis, public transportation systems could not cope with the number of people needing to travel around the country.

▲ A taxi makes its way through the streets of Ajeromi, Lagos. Poor drainage means that this area often floods in the rainy season.

▼ Oil pipelines run directly through the town of Okrika in the Niger Delta.

Oil Billions

Nigeria exports more oil than any other African country, and is a major world supplier. Two million barrels of Nigerian oil reach world markets every day, and the country's reserves could last for many more decades. Yet the huge amount of money that oil brings into Nigeria is not shared evenly around the country or being spent on ordinary Nigerians. A large chunk of oil profits has either disappeared into the private bank accounts of corrupt politicians and military rulers, or been lost through bad management.

OIL ON TROUBLED WATERS

When oil was discovered in the 1950s, Nigerians hoped it would bring prosperity. Instead, many Nigerians have grown increasingly angry about the oil industry. The people who live in the Delta, such as the Ogoni and Ijaw, have seen their land and water nearly destroyed. Pollution from oil spills has poisoned the delta's creeks and swamps. Gas flares on oil rigs disturb people's sleep and release poisons into the atmosphere. Yet locals receive little from the billions made off the land they live on. In the 1990s, the Ogoni leader Ken Saro-Wiwa, brought his people's problems to the attention of the world. The military government reacted angrily, and he and eight other activists were executed. More recently activists have taken foreign oil workers hostage and planted bombs to try to force change. Others have taken oil companies to court. In 2001, Shell was ordered to pay $1.5 billion to the Ijaw people. Finding a balance between oil production and the needs and rights of the Delta peoples is one of the biggest challenges facing oil companies and the Nigerian government.

▼ Oil spills on Ogoni land in the Niger Delta often catch fire by accident and burn for weeks.

A Bright Future?

A quarter of Africans living south of the Sahara are Nigerians. With such a large workforce, Nigeria could become a world economic power. But first, the country must break its reliance on oil and start to make money in new ways. Tourism is one growth area. Nigeria has many historic and wildlife attractions but, so far, few foreign tourists. If the government can cut corruption and crime, Nigeria will become a popular destination.

Add a Little Extra to Your Country Report!

I f you are assigned to write a report about Nigeria, you'll want to include basic information about the country, of course. The Fast Facts chart on page 8 will give you a good start. The rest of the book will give you the details you need to create a full and up-to-date paper or PowerPoint presentation. But what can you do to make your report more fun than anyone else's? If you use your imagination and dig a bit deeper into some of the topics introduced in this book, you're sure to come up with information that will make your report unique!

>Flag

Perhaps you could explain the history of Nigeria's flag, and the meanings of its colors. Go to **www.crwflags.com/fotw/flags** for more information.

>National Anthem

How about downloading Nigeria's national anthem, and playing it for your class? At **www.nationalanthems.info** you'll find what you need, including the words to the anthem, plus sheet music for the anthem. Simply pick "N" and then "Nigeria" from the list on the left-hand side of the screen, and you're on your way.

>Time Difference

If you want to understand the time difference between Nigeria and where you are, this Web site can help: **www.worldtimeserver.com**. Just pick "Nigeria" from the list on the left. If you called Nigeria right now, would you wake whomever you are calling from their sleep?

>Currency

Another Web site will convert your money into naira, the currency used in Nigeria. You'll want to know how much money to bring if you're ever lucky enough to travel to Nigeria: **www.xe.com/ucc**.

>Weather

Why not check the current weather in Nigeria? It's easy—simply go to **www.weather.com** to find out if it's sunny or cloudy, warm or cold in Nigeria right this minute! Pick "World" from the headings at the top of the page. Then search for Nigeria. Click on any city you like. Be sure to click on the tabs below the weather report for Sunrise/Sunset information, Weather Watch, and Business Travel Outlook, too. Scroll down the page for the 36-hour Forecast and a satellite weather map. Compare your weather to the weather in the Nigerian city you chose. Is this a good season, weather-wise, for a person to travel to Nigeria?

>Miscellaneous

Still want more information? Simply go to National Geographic's One-Stop Research site at **http://www.nationalgeographic.com/onestop**. It will help you find maps, photos and art, articles and information, games and features that you can use to jazz up your report.

Glossary

Archaeologist a person who studies the remains of ancient people to learn more about how people lived in the past.

Cassava the root of a shrub that is used for food. Cassava is originally from South America but is now grown in Africa and Asia. Cassava can be fried, boiled and mashed like potatoes or made into flour for dumplings.

Ceremonial a duty or ritual that is performed as a symbol of a belief or a power.

Coup the sudden removal of a government by a small group of people, often military officers.

Delta the mouth of a river where the stream splits into two or more branches. The split streams form a triangle shape called a delta for the Greek letter Δ.

Dictator a leader who has complete control over a country and does not have to be elected or re-elected to office regularly. Dictators are often cruel and corrupt.

Economy the system by which a country creates wealth through making and trading in products.

Ecosystem a community of living things and the environment they interact with; an ecosystem includes plants, animals, soil, water, and air.

Emir the leader of a Muslim community.

Ethnic group a large section of a country's population with members that share a common ancestry or background.

Exported transported and sold outside the country of origin.

Habitat a part of the environment that is suitable for certain plants and animals.

Hostage a person held prisoner for political reasons.

Humidity moisture, or water vapor, in the air.

Imported brought into the country from abroad.

Migration the annual movement of animals, such as birds, deer, or whales, from one place to another.

Nationalist a belief or political movement that celebrates a certain nation or country. Nationalists believe that their government should not be controlled by people from another country.

Peace-keeping force a military force that is sent into troublespots and war zones to prevent violence.

Republic a country that is ruled by an elected head of state, such as a president.

Savanna an area of grassland with few trees and shrubs that is found in warm parts of the world.

Silt very fine soil and clay that is carried by large rivers. As it settles to the riverbed, silt forms deep mud.

Silverback a fully-grown, adult male gorilla that has silver-gray hairs on its back and belly. A troop of gorillas is led by a silverback.

Species a type of organism; animals or plants in the same species look similar and can only breed successfully among themselves.

Treaty a written agreement between two or more countries. Treaties are made to end wars or organize trade.

Urban describes a city.

Bibliography

Graham, Ian. *Nigeria*. North Mankato, MN: Smart Apple Media, 2004.

Hamilton, Janice. *Nigeria in Pictures*. Minneapolis, MN: Lerner Publications, 2003.

Kerr, Esther. *Welcome to Nigeria*. Milwaukee, WS: Gareth Stevens, 2002.

http://news.bbc.co.uk/1/hi/world/africa/country_profiles/1064557.stm (general information)

http://www.nigeria.gov.ng/ (official government Web site)

http://www.state.gov/r/pa/ei/bgn/2836.htm (information from the U.S. State Department)

Further Information

NATIONAL GEOGRAPHIC Articles

"Memorial to a Warrior for the Environment." NATIONAL GEOGRAPHIC (April 1996): Geographica.

O' Neill, Tom. "Curse of the Black Gold: Hope and Betrayal in the Niger Delta." NATIONAL GEOGRAPHIC (February 2007): 88–117.

Web sites to explore

More fast facts about Nigeria, from the CIA (Central Intelligence Agency): https://www.cia.gov/cia/publications/factbook/geos/ni.html

Learn more about the Nok culture, the oldest civilization in Nigeria, and one of the most ancient in Africa: http://cghs.dadeschools.net/african-american/tradtional/nok.ht

Do you want to see more of what life is like on the Jos Plateau? Take a look at the photo gallery provided by the state government: http://www.plateaustategov.org/photos/index.html

Would you like to hear some Nigerian music? You can listen to the work of some of Nigeria's most popular musicians at this site: http://www.onlinenigeria.com/music

Everyone has heard of Hollywood, and perhaps you know about Bollywood, the Indian film industry—but have you heard of Nollywood? Nollywood is the nickname for Nigerian cinema. Learn more about it at: http://www.thisisnollywood.com/

See, hear

There are many ways to get a taste of life in Nigeria, such as movies, music CDs, magazines, or TV shows. You might be able to locate these:

Afrobeat
This is a form of Nigerian pop music. The most famous Afrobeat star was Fela Kuti. The music is fast and lively and is played by big bands.

Ben Okri
Okri is one of the most famous modern Nigerian writers. He was born in England, but moved to Nigeria at age nine. His most famous book is *The Famished Road* (1990).

Chris Ofili
Ofili is a British painter with Nigerian origins. His work draws on his African roots. In 1998, Ofili won the top British arts prize.

Index

Boldface indicates
illustrations.

Abuja 8, 17, 50, 56
acacias 25
Achebe, Chinua 46
Adamawa Plateau 13–14
Afrobeat 47
alafin **31**
Annang **47**
antelopes **20**, **22**, 23
ants 25, **25**
Argungu fishing competition
6–7, 7
art **44**, 45–46
see also sculpture

baboons 25
Balewa, Tafawa 37
Benin 28, 34
bronzes 34, **34**
Benue River 8, 12, 17
Biafra 53, **53**
bongos 23
Bono **52**
Borno 28
British empire 28, 36–37,
37
bronzes
Benin **34**
Ife **32**
Yoruba **31**
bushbucks 23
bush taxis 55

Calabar 16, **36**
calabashes **14**, 32
Cameroon Highlands 8, 13
cattle herders 33, **33**
Chad, Lake **13**, 30
Chappal Waddi 8
Christianity 43, 44–45
cities 15–17, 31, 32, 40,
54
city-states 33

climate 8, **8**, 12
map **8**
crocodiles 20, 24

dance **47**
deforestation 20
desert 15, **15**
diet 45
Dufana Canoe 30
duikers **22**, 23
durbars **38–39**, 39

Economic Community of
West African States
(ECOWAS) 49
economy 49, 54–55, **55**,
56–57
industry map **54**
ecosystems 20–5, **21**
education **43**
Eid al-Fitr 43
Eid el-Kabir 43
Ekiti 50
elephants 22–23, **23**
emirs 28, 33
employment 42–43, 54–56
Equiano, Olaudah 36, 46

family life 42–44
farming 12, **15**, 20, 30, **30**,
42, 45
cooperative societies
54
fishing **6–7**, 7, **13**
flooding **56**
forests 19, 20, 22–23, 46
Fulani 15, 28, **32**, 33

giraffes 23, 25
gold 33
gorillas **18–19**, 19, 22
groundnuts 37, **54**

hartebeests **20**
Hausa 15, 28, **32**, 33–34

Hausa language 40
common phrases 40
history of Nigeria 28–37, **29**
holidays 43
horses 31, 33, **33**

Ibibio **44**
Ife (Ile-Ife) 32
Igbo 32–33, 36, **44**, 45, 46,
53
Igbo language 40
common phrases 40
Igbo-Ukwu 28
Ijaw 57
independence 28, 37, 52
industry
map **54**
Islam 34, **35**, 39, 43, 44
Iwo Eleru 30

Jos Plateau 8, 12, **13**, 17,
27

Kano 15, 17, **32**, 33, **35**,
54
Sallah Durbar **38–39**, 39
Katsina 15, **15**, 33, 39
kings 28, 31
Kuti, Fela Ransome 47, **47**

Lagos 15–16, **16**, 17, 47,
56
languages 8, 40
common phrases 40
lions 20, 23
Lokoja 17

manatees 2
mangrove swamp 10–11, 24
maps
climate **8**
historical **29**
industry **54**
Niger Delta **11**
physical **9**

Credits

Picture Credits

NGIC = National Geographic Image Collection

Front Cover – Spine: Luba V. Nel/Shutterstock; Top: NGIC; Low far left: W. Robert Moore/NGIC; Low left: Mattias Klum/NGIC; Low right: Stuart Franklin/NGIC; Low far right: NGIC.

Interior – Corbis: Bernard Bisson/Sygma: 47 lo; Bettmann: 53 up; Margaret Courtney-Clark: 44 lo; William Campbell/Sygma: 50 lo: Sophie Elbaz/Sygma: 33 lo: Pascal Lauener/Reuters: 52 up; Gideon Mendell/Action Aid: 56 up; Onome Oghene/epa: 3 left, 38–39; STR/epa: 46 lo; Liba Taylor: 42 up; TH-Foto/Zefa: 30 up; Werner Forman: 2–3, 26–27, 44 up; NGIC: Anschel Collection/Bruno Piazza: 31 up; Bruno Barbey/Magnum: 2 left, 6–7, 12 lo, 16 center, 32 up Dea & Jen Bartlett: 20 lo, 24 lo; Michael Fay: 23 up; Stuart Franklin: 43 lo; Gordon Gahan: 13 up; David Hughes: 25 lo; Ed Kashi: TP, 3 right, 10 up, 11 lo, 28 up, 45 lo, 48–49, 55 up, 56 lo, 57 up; Lynn Johnson: 15 up, 33 up; A. R. Moore: 14 lo; W. Robert Moore: 5 up, 15 lo, 17 up, 31 lo, 35 lo, 36 up, 37 center, 47 up, 54 lo; Michael Nichols: 2 right, 18–19, 22 lo, 23 lo; James L. Stanfield: 34 up; The Brown Reference Group: 59 up.

For more information, please call 1-800-NGS-LINE (647-5463) or write to the following address:

NATIONAL GEOGRAPHIC SOCIETY
1145 17th Street N.W.
Washington, D.C. 20036-4688 U.S.A.

Visit the Society's Web site at
www.nationalgeographic.com/books

Library of Congress Cataloging-in-Publication Data available on request
ISBN: 978-1-4263-0124-7

Printed in the United States of America

Series design by Jim Hiscott.
The body text is set in Avenir; Knockout.
The display text is set in Matrix Script.

Front Cover—Top: Women on their way to market near Ibadan; Low Far Left: Cargo boats on the Niger River; Low Left: A cattle herder in a rain forest; Low Right: Students in class in Lagos, Nigeria; Low Far Right: The central mosque in Kano

Page 1—A young child sells baked food in Okrika in the Niger Delta; Icon image on spine, Contents page, and throughout: Textile patterns

Produced through the worldwide resources of the National Geographic Society

John M. Fahey, Jr., *President and Chief Executive Officer;* Gilbert M. Grosvenor, *Chairman of the Board;* Nina D. Hoffman, *Executive Vice President, President of Book Publishing Group*

National Geographic Staff for this Book

Nancy Laties Feresten, *Vice President, Editor-in-Chief of Children's Books*
Bea Jackson, *Director of Design and Illustration*
David M. Seager, *Art Director*
Priyanka Lamichhane, *Project Editor*
Lori Epstein, *Illustrations Editor*
Stacy Gold, Nadia Hughes, *Illustrations Research Editors*
R. Gary Colbert, *Production Director*
Lewis R. Bassford, *Production Manager*
Maryclare Tracy, Nicole Elliott, *Manufacturing Managers*
Maps, *Mapping Specialists, Ltd.*

Brown Reference Group plc. Staff for this Book

Volume Editor: Sally MacEachern
Designer: Dave Allen
Picture Manager: Becky Cox
Maps: Martin Darlinson
Artwork: Darren Awuah
Index: Ann Barrett
Senior Managing Editor: Tim Cooke
Design Manager: Sarah Williams
Children's Publisher: Anne O'Daly
Editorial Director: Lindsey Lowe

About the Author

BRIDGET GILES studied the geography and religions of Africa at the School of Oriental and African Studies (SOAS), University of London, United Kingdom. Since then, she has written and edited a number of books for children and young adults on the people, cultures, religions, and geography of Africa.

About the Consultants

BENJAMIN AKÍNTÚNDÉ OYÈTÁDÉ is a lecturer in Yoruba language and culture and Head of Department of the Languages and Cultures of Africa, School of Oriental and African Studies, University of London, United Kingdom. His research focuses on Yoruba language and culture in the Yoruba homeland in Nigeria and in the Diaspora. Dr. Oyètádé has also worked together with Victor Fashole Luke of Fourah Bay College, University of Sierra Leone to study the impact of the ten-year civil war in Sierra Leone on Krio, the national language.

MATTHEWS A. OJO is a professor of Religious Studies at the Obafemi Awolowo University, Ile-Ife, Nigeria. His research focuses on Pentecostal movements and contemporary society in Africa, new religious movements, religion and sexuality among youth, and the media and religion in Nigeria. His most recent book is *End Time Army: Charismatic Movements in Modern Nigeria* (2006). Professor Ojo has carried out research in British and American universities, and in 2002 taught at Harvard University, Cambridge, USA.